The Family That Prays Together *Stays Together*

Train up a child in the way he should go: and when he is old, he will not depart from it.

Proverbs 22:6

The Family That Prays Together *Stays Together*

Train up a child in the way he should go: and when he is old, he will not depart from it.

Proverbs 22:6

The Family That Prays Together *Stays Together*

Train up a child in the way he should go: and when he is old, he will not depart from it.

Proverbs 22:6

The Family That Prays Together
Stays Together

Train up a child in the way he should go: and when he is old, he will not depart from it.

Proverbs 22:6

© 2022 Broadman Church Supplies
Brentwood, TN Printed in the USA.

BROADMAN CHURCH SUPPLIES

Scripture from KJV
840154557902